ADVANCE PRAISE

Through participant observation and rigorous study of social formations within capitalist regimes but outside capitalist values, Matthews and Waitzkin draw a series of examples across countries that foster the possibilities of a better and more just future in the housing, healthcare, and income maintenance spaces. Coming from a colony long subjected to racial capitalism, Puerto Rico, and having seen the dismantling of a solidarity healthcare project by privatization and the flourishing of community-based initiatives in resistance, this work connects our experiences with a larger context of solidarity, care, and love. It gives us ideas and invites a reflection on what internal and external forces might influence and contribute to another possible world.

— **Nylca Munoz**, lawyer at LLM Program, Harvard Law School, 2025, and American Bar Foundation Access to Justice Scholar focusing on health justice and decolonization in Puerto Rico.

Welfare for a Humane Future is clearly written in style, evocative in its thinking, international in scope, and fearless in whacking through dogma while centering compassion in community. Drawing deeply from an interdisciplinary literature and participant observation, not only as scholars, but at one time for the authors as welfare recipients and low income themselves. The pamphlet manifesto here is essential reading for everyone from revolutionaries to policy makers, journalists, union members, social workers, scholars, and welfare recipients. In short order, in the time it takes to wait for an appointment with a case officer, Matthews and Waitzkin hammer out many of the exciting brass tacks of a variety of bottom-up-led post-capitalist social welfare systems, some already in motion in communities, collectives, confederations, committees, communes, councils, and co-ops around the world. We learn here that housing, community health, and income support are all cooperative opportunities, open to everyone everywhere prepared to fight for them.

— **Rob Wallace**, author of *Big Farms Make Big Flu* and *The Fault in Our SARS*; organizer, Pandemic Research for the People

This pamphlet offers clear solutions for moving towards a post-capitalist society. What stood out to me is its emphasis on key values: solidarity, collectivism, love, and altruism, which align with ongoing efforts to address the harms of racial capitalism through reparative justice. However, even reparations must be guided by these core values and integrated into broader efforts to move beyond capitalism. The pamphlet's vision for post-capitalist welfare systems aligns with abolitionist frameworks, prioritizing structural solutions, mutual aid, and community-led decision-making. Its action-oriented approach and examples of "post-capitalist enclaves/communities" within capitalist societies provide a blueprint for movements, researchers, and communities. On a global scale, these values could also shape post-capitalist aid systems.

— **Tinashe Goronga**, a medical doctor in Zimbabwe, passionate about understanding and addressing structural determination of health; one of the organizers for Equalhealth's global campaign against racism

....

Welfare for a Humane Future is the hope – and primer – we need now. With concrete examples to spur our movements for community-driven safety, self-determination and joy, it is an instructive guide for how we can survive and thrive past capitalism's expiration date. The U.S. is arguably the center of our current hegemonic capitalist empire of control over Earth's resources. For someone like me living in the U.S. as it collapses, David and Howard's pamphlet breathes life into the overwhelming dread, the chaos and the despair I'm experiencing right now. But no matter where you live in the world or the current political and economic predicament in which you find yourself, *Welfare for a Humane Future* has guiding examples from several countries where people have built self-governing communities of safety and wellbeing during an analogous upheaval. It's a must-read for anyone who is newly using the phrase "we keep each other safe," to understand exactly how it can be done.

— **Melody Wells,** independent journalist, fundraiser and organizer focusing on LGBTQ communities in New Mexico

....

This short book is an important tonic for our times, as we confront the hideous emergence of Trump 2.0 and the increasing political drift to far right authoritarian capitalism. The examples it offers of communal efforts to create post-capitalist economies of 'love, care, and compassion' provide some needed hope that, even when higher political orders become increasingly toxic, local-level activism can keep the ideals of ecojust alternatives alive. The authors usefully Identify some of the steps needed to initiate a post-capitalist welfare that is true to its roots meaning: living 'well' and being 'fair'.

— **Ronald Labonté**, Professor Emeritus, School of Epidemiology and Public Health, University of Ottawa

Moved by "the optimism of the will", in Gramscian terms, the authors of this much-needed pamphlet call for a radical change towards a post-capitalist society. As they convincingly argue, moving beyond the welfare state of racial capitalism is key to such transformation. Through well-documented historical cases and inspiring contemporary examples from around the world, they show how sprouts of such new society already exist, and how welfare can be the plot on which strong community networks are woven to secure housing, income, and healthcare while regenerating love, care, and solidarity.

— **Chiara Bodini**, Center for International and Intercultural Health, Bologna, Italy, and People's Health Movement

Welfare for a Humane Future critiques the racialized and exploitative nature of capitalist welfare systems while envisioning a community-driven alternative rooted in love, solidarity, and participatory democracy. Drawing on real-world examples the book outlines practical strategies for equitable housing, healthcare, and income systems that empower people rather than corporations. A must-read for activists and scholars, it offers a transformative blueprint for building post-capitalist welfare solutions through mutual aid and collective governance.

— **Tony Harrison**, Black Canadian writer, community organizer, and host of the podcast Actually Existing Socialism

Capitalism has brought us to the brink of ecocide and human extinction. Matthews and Waitzkin urge us to step back from the brink by re-imagining human welfare from the class perspective of working people, especially those of color. They draw upon Marxist and anarchist currents – especially the economic thought of Che Guevara – and examine efforts to achieve post-capitalist human welfare around the world. The billionaires won't like it, but the rest of us can be happier in such a de-growth world, which fosters welfare services outside the capitalist state.

— **Seiji Yamada**, professor of family medicine and community health at the University of Hawai'i

Reading this pamphlet, I learned about the rich experience of many countries, and it reminds me of the efforts in the Philippine experience. The Philippine progressive and revolutionary movements have been doing so much in creating a post-capitalist society. We do this in the framework of National Democracy: Land for the tillers, just wage for the workers, basic social services for everyone. Take back the wealth from the 1%, pretty much. Take control of the government, build a new government for the people, by the people. Filipinos know very well we need a new society that only comes from painstaking efforts to "shake off capitalism's imprint" as this fascinating pamphlet says, a true revolution.

— **Arcelita Imasa**, activist and family medicine practitioner
  in the Philippines and Hawai'i

....

In their powerful short book, David Matthews and Howard Waitzkin analyze how racial capitalism perpetuates economic exploitation, blunts the human potential for cooperation, kindness, and compassion, and leads to inadequate social welfare policies. The authors describe alternative models of governance based on community solidarity, using current successful examples from several countries around the world. The post-capitalist future envisioned by the authors, centered on radical democracy and local decision-making rather than top-down state control, is hopeful and pragmatic. This exciting work will encourage readers to rethink and transform welfare beyond the unsuccessful and demeaning structures managed by the capitalist welfare state.

— **Claudia Chaufan**, Associate Professor, Health Policy &
  Global Health, York University, Toronto, Canada

Welfare
for a
Humane Future

Moving Beyond the Welfare State of Racial Capitalism

David Matthews & Howard Waitzkin

Daraja Press

Published by
Daraja Press
https://darajapress.com
Wakefield, Quebec, Canada
2025

ISBN: 9781998309528 (softcover)
ISBN: 9781998309535 (ePub)

© 2025 David Matthews & Howard Waitzkin
Moving Beyond Capitalism – Now! Series editor: Howard Waitzkin

Cover and book design by Kate McDonnell

Library and Archives Canada Cataloguing in Publication

Title: Welfare for a humane future : moving beyond the welfare state of racial
   capitalism / David Matthews & Howard Waitzkin.
Names: Matthews, David (Professor), author. | Waitzkin, Howard, author
Description: Includes bibliographical references.
Identifiers: Canadiana (print) 20250161699 | Canadiana (ebook) 20250161710 |
   ISBN 9781998309528 (softcover) | ISBN 9781998309535 (EPUB)
Subjects: LCSH: Social justice. | LCSH: Social policy. | LCSH: Welfare state.
   | LCSH: Public welfare. | LCSH: Income distribution. | LCSH: Capitalism—Social
   aspects. | LCSH: Race relations— Economic aspects.
Classification: LCC HM671 .M38 2025 | DDC 361.6/1—dc23

Contents

Moving Beyond the Welfare State of Racial Capitalism

What does welfare mean under capitalism? What is the welfare that we seek? Despite their importance, these questions about welfare rarely arise in critiques of capitalism or strategies of revolutionary transformation. Seeking the answers involves looking closely at how welfare works under capitalism, specifically under racial capitalism. Envisioning a future for welfare depends on examining how welfare can change within the broader transformation of racial capitalism.

Why "racial" capitalism? Today, as during its entire history, capitalism's prosperity relies on the exploitation of the majority by a minority. Few of us are immune from having to work for a living, earning a wage for ourselves, and amassing wealth for an elite who control society's economic resources. This fundamental division of social class lies at the heart of how capitalism works. But capitalism also is replete with other sources of oppression, discrimination, and exploitation.

In the title and throughout this work, we emphasize the racial character of capitalism. Racism and socially constructed race, inherently entangled with social class, infuse capitalism. This entangling results in an intertwined web of exploitative experiences and circumstances. The intersection of class and race defines global capitalism in the twenty-first century. But from its origins, capitalism has always been racialized: a global system organized by, and for the benefit of, a predominantly white capitalist elite.[1] Direct and indirect military control of

---

1 Lilia D. Monzo, "Colonialism, Migration, Pandemic: The Immutable Evidence that Capitalism is Racist and Misogynist," *Monthly Review* 72, no. 3 (2020): 48-63.

overseas markets by imperial nations underpins racial capitalism and has done so from its beginning. In *Capital*, Marx clarified the interconnections among capitalism, imperialism, and structural racism, manifested most clearly by initiating the slavery and genocide of indigenous peoples. Marx called these events the "rosy dawn of capitalism."[2]

The racial character of capitalism manifests throughout its history, including the present moment. In the lived experience of economic dependency, workers in subjugated countries endure intense exploitation and deprivation. Within the imperial nations, ethnic minorities fare little better as victims of heightened exploitation.[3] As Black anarchist Lorenzo Kom'boa Ervin asserts, racism operates as "a class doctrine, used by the state for social control of workers of color."[4]

Socially constructed race divides working people at the level of consciousness, and structural racism provides the institutional framework through which this division occurs. As Michael Zweig clarifies, the precarity of jobs in the capitalist labor market has meant that, in the pursuit of security and advantage, white working people intermittently have demanded the exclusion of people of color from the competitive search for work, housing, and education.[5] Due to the unpredictability of the labor market, divisions and hatred often have arisen in the relationships among working people of varying ethnic backgrounds. These conditions have ensured that suspicion

2 Karl Marx, *Capital*, volume 1, chapter 31, https://www.marxists.org/archive/marx/works/1867-c1/ch31.htm; Eduardo Galeano, *The Open Veins of Latin America* (New York: Monthly Review Press, 1997), Part I.

3 Charisse Burden-Stelley, "Modern U.S. Racial Capitalism: Some Theoretical Insights," *Monthly Review* 72, no. 3 (2020): 8-20; Zophia Edwards, "Racial Capitalism and COVID-19," *Monthly Review* 72, No. 10 (2021): 21-31.

4 Lorenzo Kon'boa Ervin, *Anarchism and the Black Revolution* (London: Pluto Press, 2021), 90. See also the discussion of Ervin's work in Atticus Bagby-Williams, et al. *Black Anarchism and the Black Radical Tradition* (Wakefield, Quebec, Canada: Daraja Press, 2023).

5 Michael Zweig, *Class, Race, and Gender: Challenging the Injuries and Divisions of Capitalism* (Oakland: PM Press, 2023).

prevails between people of color and white members of the labor force. This division, as Ervin makes clear, undermines working and living standards for all members of the workforce, exacerbating poverty and exploitation. As white workers confront their ethnic minority counterparts, this antagonism challenges any hope of the working class uniting to oppose the authority of capitalist elites. "As long as workers are fighting one another," Ervin argues, "capitalist class rule is secure."[6]

The racial character of capitalism also extends to welfare, which comprises the widely variable financial and other material assistance that people "in need" receive from agencies of government. Such government agencies together comprise the capitalist welfare state. Welfare plays an important part in tethering us to an exploitative system of wage labor. Racial capitalism cannot sustain itself through force alone. Institutions and social processes, including elements of both coercion and persuasion, elicit consent to our own exploitation.

During and after World War II, the welfare state's expansion became crucial for capitalism's growth and stability. Critiques of welfare focus on its advantages for capitalism, framing the welfare state as an instrumental apparatus sustaining and reproducing capitalism and its injustices.[7] Welfare states have helped solidify oppression and discriminatory ideologies, including those of racism. New Deal welfare reforms during the Great Depression in the United States reinforced racial divisions. Social security legislation, Zweig illustrates, precluded from eligibility those occupations mainly conducted by Black workers. Similarly, minimum wage legislation and regulations limiting the length of the working week again excluded those occupations.[8]

6 Ervin, *Anarchism and the Black Revolution*, 81-82.
7 See Ian Gough, *The Political Economy of the Welfare State* (London: Macmillan, 1979); James O'Connor, *The Fiscal Crisis of the State* (London: St. James, 1973); Claus Offe, *Contradictions of the Welfare State* (Cambridge: MIT Press, 1984).
8 Zweig, *Class, Race, and Gender*, 169-170.

Many New Deal reforms, therefore, hinged on continuing discrimination and racism. As well as reinforcing division by providing little to no security for Black and ethnic minority workers, these reforms also fostered a pool of workers available for greater exploitation in comparison to their white counterparts. The experience of claiming welfare benefits is also often punitive for ethnic minority groups, reflecting social control by the state. Underpinned by racist labeling and stereotypes of welfare recipients, frequent calls by ruling elites and by conservative-influenced members of the working class favor cuts in the provision of welfare benefits. Ideological constructions about welfare propagated by ruling elites have reinforced racist beliefs and divisions within the working class.

Beyond the capitalist welfare state. The state usually bolsters capitalism, a position that must remain central to any critique, but the class struggle between working people and capitalism's dominant class has consistently shaped the welfare state. Although embraced by economic and political elites, the welfare state is also an instrument that working people have grasped to defend themselves against their exploitation. Despite the discrimination reflected in and reinforced by welfare states towards working people of color, a contradiction of the welfare state is that its history shows generations of workers who have recognized its importance. Workers' demands for welfare provision can help combat the economic and social aggression of free-market capitalism.[9]

The purpose here is to examine what a post-capitalist welfare system might look like. Such a system would meet the needs of working people, not the needs of capitalist corporations, and move beyond the oppressive and discriminatory tendencies that have characterized welfare under capitalism. Rather than occupying part of an oppressive capitalist state,

9 David Matthews, *The Class Struggle and Welfare: Social Policy Under Capitalism* (New York: Monthly Review Press, 2025), chapters 4-5.

this new approach to welfare flourishes under popular control, as it both depends on and promotes solidarity among working people.

This pamphlet focuses on the values and principles underpinning welfare in a post-capitalist society. Such a society provides love, care, and compassion. These values radically transform how we behave toward each other, resulting in the establishment of new social relationships. No longer imprisoned and governed by hierarchy, class relations, discrimination, and oppression, we enjoy the freedom to act toward each other as equals.

Analytic framework. Crucial to the enactment of such values is the creation of a post-capitalist welfare system. Examples present how, in practice, such a system operates. Information about these examples comes from our own participation as activists and/or in-depth study of writings and presentations by people who have participated directly in community-level social welfare processes that move beyond racial capitalism. Our analytic framework to interrogate the examples is inductive, based on a participatory approach that identifies the elements of welfare that move beyond the constraints of racial capitalism and the capitalist welfare state.

Applying such an analytic framework can prove challenging. For instance, self-reports by leaders tend to highlight positive achievements and downplay disappointments or failures. Such slanted descriptions slide into propaganda. Reports by external observers can contain unstated biases that lead to favorable or less favorable interpretations, depending on political values, academic or journalistic practices, and financial or political conflicts of interest.

So, our analytic framework and methods try to address these challenges, at least in part. Some of our examples of post-capitalist welfare systems come from our visits and/or lived experiences in several countries, regions of countries, and localities. Our approach usually involves participant observation with community-based, governmental, or health organizations rather than more detached approaches using interviews only. To supplement our direct observations or to substitute for them in locations that we did not visit, we draw from books, articles, and reports that focus on one or more of the selected geographical areas. We also have conducted internet searches and have investigated online databases that include journal articles, books, and some documents released by government agencies, non-government organizations, international financial institutions, and international health organizations. For our own direct observations and information coming from other sources, we explicitly try to identify bias through a requirement that the reports include criticisms and limitations as well as positive accomplishments. We and others find that this approach filters out most unbalanced or inaccurate findings.

Examining housing, health, and income maintenance, we consider how to organize and deliver post-capitalist welfare services that aim to meet everyone's needs. Such a welfare system anchors itself in communities where we live and share our lives. The creation and maintenance of welfare practices happen through participatory decision-making rather than within a hierarchically organized welfare state. This participatory framework aims to assure that welfare services actually do meet people's needs in practice. We offer this information and analysis not as a corner on the truth of post-capitalist welfare but rather as a step to imagine a transformation of welfare based on actual experiences in many places around the world.[10] In this

10 In general, the examples focus on countries, or regions of countries, that still retain overall capitalist political-economic systems. These examples show how attempts to move from capitalist to post-capitalist welfare systems are happening within currently capitalist societies. The welfare systems of societies that have moved to "actually existing socialism" through violent revolutions overthrowing capitalism also deserve clarification, which we are trying to do in other work. A draft is available by communication with Howard Waitzkin (waitzkin@unm.edu): Howard Waitzkin and Sapna Mishra, "The Transition from Racial Capitalism to Post-Capitalist Health and Welfare Systems." That manuscript focuses especially on municipal governments and community-based organizations in post-revolutionary societies,

effort, we welcome constructive criticism and feedback.

Overview of our argument. We begin by emphasizing a fundamental change in values that happens by acting to implement components of a post-capitalist society and welfare system now. Capitalism is permeated by greed, selfishness, individualism, and a drive to accumulate wealth. Even if we object to these values, we frequently feel we have no choice but to act this way if we hope to survive under capitalism. Such survival, we assume, depends on getting a job, buying a car, and affording the mortgage or rent.

We argue that it is time to turn our backs on capitalist values and, as far as possible, to begin leading our lives as though we already live in a post-capitalist society to which we aspire. Instead of capitalist values, we support people acting in accordance with care, love, solidarity, and collectivism. With reference to the philosophical and practical positions of authors like Erich Fromm, Erik Olin Wright, and Che Guevara, we advocate for strong communities that manifest cohesion and solidarity so these values can flourish. Within cohesive communities, we need communal institutions that promote and reinforce the values of love, care, and solidarity. Among communal institutions, those that process welfare services figure among the most important.

The next stage of our argument focuses on democratic decision-making. We aim to construct a democratic environment that supports the development of communal welfare institutions. Popular empowerment allows community members to take control of communal institutions. The goal is to build local communes and assemblies as centers for local democratic decision-making. Here, we embrace the theories and practices of Murray Bookchin and Lorenzo Kom'boa Ervin, as well as the accomplishments of Cooperation Jackson in Mississippi.

....

for instance People's Power (Poder Popular) and the Committees for the Defense of the Revolution, the Federation of Cuban Women, and related organizations in Cuba.

Our current social reality contains the basis for such fundamental changes, so we don't need to start from scratch. In the next stage of our argument, we illustrate that within our communities today already exist democratic institutions and organizations that we can understand as spaces free from capitalist values. Specifically, we can already see the foundations of a post-capitalist welfare system. We can pay attention to the many organizations and institutions already established upon the principles of mutual aid and collectivism as sources of inspiration. These organizations and institutions offer foundations from which we can build a post-capitalist welfare system located in communities and reflect the values of love, care, and solidarity.

All the post-capitalist welfare systems that we consider in this pamphlet developed or are developing from roots in societies with capitalist political-economic systems. These examples show that, within the oppressive context of racial capitalism, spaces for building post-capitalist welfare emerge in communal or other collective forms of mutual aid and economic relationships based on solidarity. The examples that we describe and analyze – Cooperation Jackson, Rojava, Venezuela, Zapatista liberated zones in Mexico, and other efforts in countries like the United States, Canada, and the United Kingdom – all involve changes that began initially within capitalist regimes. To differing extents, they all remain embedded, at least in part, within capitalist contexts. Even for Cuba, the only post-capitalist society that we consider here whose transformation occurred through a violent revolution, the origins of community-based decision-making processes and mutual aid originated through local organizing efforts. It grew gradually both before and after Cuba's violent revolution. In short, the roots of post-capitalist welfare within capitalist contexts warrant more recognition in the ongoing, broader struggle to overcome racial capitalism.

Our argument concludes with additional concrete examples, both contemporary and from the recent past, that clarify alternative ways to deliver post-capitalist welfare. Focusing on housing, health, and income maintenance, we can already see ways to provide these services through mutual aid and cooperative institutions. Many of these efforts ground themselves firmly within communities, allowing those who use them and support their delivery to influence their management. As inspiration we again point to contemporary developments in Cooperation Jackson, Cooperation Humboldt, coop housing schemes in Britain, as well as recent historical interventions providing welfare services by organizations such as the Black Panther Party and Young Lords in the United States.

Humanity and Love

K arl Marx was a great economist, but at the heart of his
ideas was a deep concern for the suffering of humanity.
As countless lives drowned in a sea of poverty, he lashed out at
the degradation that capitalism wrought upon people. He was
acutely aware that despair gripped individuals who were dominated by a society where exploitation and oppression were
rampant. Revolutionary Marxist Che Guevara saw clearly the
empathy permeating Marx's writings, arguing that Marx was
"a humane man whose capacity for affection extended to all
those suffering throughout the world."[11]

Ideas of justice, equality, democracy, and freedom foster
deep concern and love for humanity. "The true revolutionary," as Guevara further asserted, "is guided by great feelings
of love."[12] Our love for both neighbor and stranger drives
radical social change. Love is at the forefront in one of the
most important social movements in recent years, Black Lives
Matter (BLM). Co-founder Opal Tometi articulates this point,
"We're a movement that is ultimately fueled by love."[13] African
American feminist and activist bell hooks asserts that the need
to express love is essential to challenging inequality, power,
and privilege. Loving ourselves and behaving towards others
with love, hooks notes, we can create environments where our
collective emotional strength nurtures the spiritual well-being

11 Ernesto Che Guevara, *Marx and Engels: A Biographical Introduction* (Melbourne: Ocean Press, 2008), 59.
12 Che Guevara, "Socialism and Man in Cuba," in *Che Guevara Reader: Writings on Guerrilla Strategy, Politics and Revolution,* ed. David Deutschmann (Melbourne: Ocean Press, 1997), 211.
13 Brian McNeill, "Black Lives Matter movement created out of love, co-founder says at VCU," *VCU News*, April 4, 2016, https://news.vcu.edu/article/black_lives_matter_movement_created_out_of_love_cofounder_says

of everyone and empowers us to struggle collectively against injustice.[14]

Exploitation and oppression shape our lives. When exploited, we become alienated from ourselves and each other. Exploitation wrenches us from our humanity, dulling our experience of being human. Often, we lack the capacity or opportunity to express love towards each other on an everyday basis. For this reason, we must break down barriers of alienation and create a system that allows for love and humanity to flourish.

As Marxist psychoanalyst Erich Fromm made clear, the meaning of humanity does not lie in biological needs, as important as they are. The most essential needs are rooted in the human condition. For Fromm, these needs include the ability to relate to others and feel loved by them, creativity, a sense of belonging, a positive sense of identity, and a framework of meaning.[15] Capitalism, however, thwarts the satisfaction of these needs.[16]

14 bell hooks, *Sisters of the Yam: Black Women and Self-Recovery* (New York: Routledge, 2015).

15 Erich Fromm, *The Sane Society* (London: Routledge, 2002), 14.

16 Fromm, *The Sane Society*, 76.

Community and Solidarity

Experiencing oppression and exploitation, we are saying, corrupts what it means to be human. Values such as competition, individualism, and greed prevail under capitalism and influence how we behave, as well as how social institutions operate. The dominance of these values creates barriers among people, especially if they must compete with each other for jobs, food, housing, and other items needed for survival. Such real or perceived competition leads to the racism that lies at the core of racial capitalism. Even within socially constructed racial groups, we become atomized members of society, viewing each other as obstacles to our progress and development. Under capitalism, the ideal individual is someone with an entrepreneurial spirit guided by self-reliance, self-improvement, and individual resilience.[17] Celebration of the individual, however, means that bonds of solidarity, collectivism, love, and altruism, which form the basis of community, become weaker. But meaningful community is crucial for meeting our needs as humans and must be front and center in our fight to build a post-capitalist society.

What do we mean by community? In his last book, *How To Be an Anti-Capitalist in the Twenty-First Century*, Erik Olin Wright refers to acts of support during everyday life. Community expresses "the principle that people ought to cooperate with each other... from a real commitment to the well-being of others and a sense of moral obligation that it is right to do so."[18] Embracing Wright's definition, we can argue

17 Andreas Chatzidakis, Jamie Hakim, Jo Littler, Catherine Rottenberg, and Lynne Segal, *The Care Manifesto: The Politics of Interdependence* (London: Verso, 2020), 2-4.
18 Erik Olin Wright, *How to be an Anticapitalist in the Twenty-First Century* (London: Verso, 2021), 18.

that community is founded on care and love. As members of a community, we all share a commitment to supporting each other's wellbeing. Membership in a community gives us an opportunity to develop our full humanity. Guevara also supported this view, claiming that "opportunities for self-expression and making oneself felt in the social organism are infinitely greater.... the individual will reach total consciousness as a social being, which is equivalent to the full realization as a human creature."[19] Experiencing the supportive nature of community, where collective values of solidarity, collectivism, love, and altruism flourish, allows every one of us the greatest opportunity to develop our emotional, social, and intellectual capacities to their fullest potential. To achieve this aim, social institutions must support the growth of the community in this sense, as well as the collective rather than individual values that form the basis of meaningful community.

19 Guevara, "Socialism and Man in Cuba," 205.

Institutionalizing Collective Values

Establishing alternative values that oppose the destructive principles that govern our lives under racial capitalism becomes a crucial goal. With rare exceptions, however, the efforts of both nonviolent and violent revolutions to build new societies based on anti-capitalist values ultimately proved unsuccessful or mostly reverted to capitalist values, even though official descriptions name the societies socialist or communist.

Utopian socialists of the eighteenth and nineteenth centuries firmly believed in the possibility of transforming both society and individuals. The Welsh industrialist and socialist Robert Owen, for example, vehemently embraced the ideal of a malleable human character. Good education, enhanced working conditions, and favorable circumstances to live one's life, he insisted, would create ideal conditions for individuals to develop progressive social values and behaviors. To prove this point, by purchasing an existing township in 1825 in southern Indiana and renaming it New Harmony, Owen sought to establish a community of cooperation and equality. But, within two years, this experiment mostly failed. Disagreement among residents regarding values that should be promoted, as well as anger about the perceived unwillingness of some participants to take their communal responsibilities seriously, led to disunity.[20]

20 Marx presented a balanced analysis and critique of Owen and his supporters at multiple places in *Capital*, volume 1, and other works. Karl Marx, *Capital, volume 1,* especially chapters 10 and 15, https://www.marxists.org/archive/marx/works/download/pdf/Capital-Volume-I.pdf. See also Richard Gunderman, "Robert Owen, born 250 years ago, tried to use his wealth to perfect humanity in a radically equal society," *The Conversation*, May 11, 2021, https://theconversation.com/robert-owen-born-250-years-ago-tried-to-use-his-wealth-to-perfect-humanity-in-a-radically-equal-society-158402

A century later, similar efforts characterized communist aspirations. In Cuba, for a communist society to develop, Guevara asserted, "it is necessary, simultaneous with the new material foundations, to build the new man."[21] The success of a socialist society required a very different social character from that developed under capitalism. Yet, the new man failed to emerge as Guevara hoped. Arguably, although Cuba's mass organizations promoted this shift of values in local communities, the overall failure happened because the effort comprised mostly a top-down initiative imposed upon the population by the officially post-capitalist state.

Ernesto "Che" Guevara at left, in Cuba

While transforming values is essential for creating a post-capitalist society, its success depends on its impetus coming from within the community. It must be a bottom-up aspiration that spreads among the people, not imposed upon us by a state apparatus. Communal institutions, with their origins in our own communities and under our collective authority, support more organic expressions of care and concern for each other.

---

21 Guevara, "Socialism and Man in Cuba." "New person" would be a better translation now.

Community institutions based on love, compassion, and solidarity can improve the likelihood that we experience meaningful relationships with each other in a post-capitalist context. In a study of communalism, Eirik Eiglad clarifies the importance of these organizations for radical social change, arguing that "a rational society will encourage solidarity and humaneness through its institutions and culture." The process gives rise to caring and empathetic individuals and behavior.[22]

Among many recent examples of communalism and the post-capitalist solidarity economy, Cooperation Humboldt has tried to implement this model. Established in Eureka, California, in 2018, the organization's primary goal is to build a community based on solidarity, collectivism, equality, and sustainability while rejecting exploitation, oppression, and prejudice. To achieve this goal, Cooperation Humboldt prioritizes the establishment of solidarity structures based on facilitating expressions of care. "We believe it is possible to create new institutions that incentivize cooperation, love, compassion, and kindness." For all involved, the overarching aim of creating these institutions is to enhance dramatically the well-being of everyone in the community.[23] Of all the institutions vital to this process, those that deliver welfare services are some of the most important for spreading the values of love, care, and solidarity. In Cooperation Humboldt, these services focus on food access and sovereignty, housing, health and mental health services, education, small business development, and disaster responses, especially for wildfires and the COVID-19 pandemic.

22 Eirik Eiglad, *Communalism as Alternative* (Porsgrunn, Norway: New Compass Press, 2014), 32.
23 David Cobb, Ruthi Engelke, Marina Lopez, Tamara MacFarland, Tobin McKee, Sabrina Miller, Oscar Mogollon, Argy Munoz, and Ron White, "Cooperation Humboldt: A Case Study," in *Jackson Rising Redux: Lessons on Building the Future in the Present*, eds. Kali Akuno and Matt Meyer (Oakland: PM Press, 2023), 321. We consider Cooperation Jackson, which provided the main influence for Cooperation Humboldt, further below.

Alongside what welfare services provide, the importance of a radical welfare system stems from how welfare institutions deliver and organize services. Their operations focus on cooperation and mutual aid. This focus enhances our attempts to create communities built upon the values of solidarity and collectivism and demonstrates care for all community members. Radical welfare services support our actions based on mutual concern for others.

Communal Control and Participatory Democracy, With Examples

Community-based institutions are necessary to solidify and institutionalize values of love, care, and solidarity and to strengthen communities themselves. Because these institutions are so important for a post-capitalist society, the political infrastructure must exist locally to ensure their development and maintenance over time. One key purpose of community-based institutions is to organize and deliver services that comprise "welfare" in the capitalist welfare state. However, in the post-capitalist context, such services become more sustainable, nurturing, and responsive to varying local needs.

Radically transferring authority from the federal and regional levels to the community level is crucial to creating communal institutions, including those that make up a post-capitalist welfare system. For such a transition, popular empowerment at the community level is essential. As Eiglad contends, local empowerment is the demand upon which all other demands depend.[24] Success in building a post-capitalist welfare system hinges on establishing a system of governance that places democratic authority within our hands. Political decision-making must move from the administrative grasp of a distant welfare state, still functioning as part of a capitalist state and exercised by distant "representatives" who engage in policymaking supposedly on our behalf. The center of political authority moves to each community, characterized by direct democracy in which everyone can choose to participate

24 Eiglad, *Communalism as Alternative*, 76.

An advocate of libertarian socialism, Murray Bookchin developed principles of communalism that offer a blueprint for grassroots democracy and equality. Bookchin's writings influenced the Rojava revolution.

directly in decision-making. To make this goal a reality, a robust system of democratic infrastructure operates at the municipal level. Local assemblies and communes play a significant role in transferring political authority to the community.

A vision of communal politics that provides much hope is the model of democratic communalism, which has come to fruition in several influential revolutionary transformations. The work of Murray Bookchin and comrades, who passionately argued in favor of face-to-face decision-making through municipal assemblies, has inspired these transformations.[25] Forums of direct democracy, such as assemblies and communes, become centers of policymaking where all members of a community can debate and decide. Decisions and policies relating to health care, education, housing, food

25 Murray Bookchin, *The Next Revolution: Popular Assemblies and the Promise of Direct Democracy* (London: Verso, 2015); *From Urbanization to Cities: The Politics of Democratic Municipalism* (Chico, CA: AK Press, 2021); *Remaking Society: A New Ecological Politics* (Chico, CA: AK Press, 2023).

production and distribution, and the environment, among other components of social welfare, happen through participation in local assemblies.

So that communities can stand strong together and do not remain isolated in attempts to achieve fundamental changes, collaborative arrangements unite separate communities and local assemblies. As advocated by Bookchin, rather than a collection of disparate and divergent institutions, a network of councils unites local assemblies. With elected representatives from each assembly, the councils coordinate and administer policies decided by each assembly. With no separate political authority, the councils support and implement the assemblies' policies, rather than imposing them from above. This process facilitates interdependence among the assemblies, which share resources and procedures.[26]

Rojava

Communal governance has underpinned the cause of Kurdish liberation, especially in Rojava, a mostly Kurdish region in northern Syria. In Rojava, the main source for principles of communalism was Abdullah Öcalan, a historical leader of the Kurdish independence movement. Öcalan initiated a concept and practice of democratic confederalism, a system of democratic self-organization with the features of a confederation based on the principles of autonomy, direct democracy, environmentalism, feminism, multiculturalism, self-defense, self-governance, and elements of a sharing economy.[27]

Öcalan's aim was to bring together the peoples of the Middle East in a confederation of democratic, multicultural, and ecological communes. Since 1999, during Öcalan's imprisonment by the government of Turkey, which continues to this day, he read widely. He succeeded in writing and publishing

26 Bookchin, The Next Revolution, 75-76.
27 Abdullah Öcalan, Democratic Confederalism, translated by International Initiative Freedom for Abdullah Öcalan (London: Transmedia Publishing, 2011), 28

Abdullah Öcalan, founding member of the Kurdistan Workers' Party,
whose theory of Democratic Confederalism laid the foundation
for Rojava's democratic revolution.

several books that have guided the Rojava revolution and have
inspired supporters in many countries. Among other influ-
ences, these writings applied some of Bookchin's reflections
on social ecology, municipalism, and a vision of communal
governance that combines elements of anarchism and socialism. This approach proposes ethical principles to replace a
society's propensity for hierarchy and domination with that of
democracy and freedom.[28] The communes take responsibility
for providing welfare services.

Adopted by the Kurdistan Workers Party (PKK) in 2005,
Öcalan's project represented a major ideological shift in the
Kurdish nationalist movement, once engaged in the armed
struggle for an independent state, to go beyond the notion of a
nation-state. In addition to the PKK, Öcalan's internationalist
project was also well received by its Syrian counterpart, the
Party of Democratic Union (PYD), which became the first

28 Steven Best, "Murray Bookchin's Theory of Social Ecology," *Organization &
Environment* 11,3 (1998): 334-53.

organization in the world to found a post-capitalist society based on principles of democratic confederalism. On January 6, 2014, the cantons of Rojava in Syrian Kurdistan "confederated" into linked, autonomous municipalities adopting a social contract that established a decentralized, non-hierarchical, post-capitalist society based on principles of direct democracy, feminism, ecology, cultural pluralism, participatory politics, economic cooperativism, and protection of human rights.[29]

Inspired partly by Bookchin's ideas of participatory governance, a dual structure of governance has emerged in Rojava. Communes, neighborhood and district assemblies, and regional councils all hold the authority to debate and act upon issues regarding the economy, women's rights and concerns, defense, justice, and welfare functions such as education, housing, food production and distribution, health and mental health services, and care for disabled people. The participatory structures coexist with governmental infrastructure at the municipal level. Municipal government functions as a kind of low-level state that facilitates decisions made through democratic processes within the participatory structures.

The Rojava revolution remains at an early stage and faces challenges stemming from external threats and internal contradictions. Turkey, which consistently opposes Kurdish autonomy, has attacked areas of Rojava with intermittent military invasions and terrorist episodes. Internal contradictions stem from trying to create new economic structures of solidarity during a transition in which elements of capitalism persist. Moving fully beyond the capitalist state remains a long-term aspiration, but the attempt to establish institutions of communal democracy working alongside a transformed governmental apparatus continues. Within this system, the municipality becomes subordinate to district councils, whose members the neighborhood

29 Thomas Schmidinger, *Rojava: Revolution, War and the Future of Syria's Kurds* (London: Pluto Press, 2018).

Prioritising direct democracy, the revolution in Rojava is based upon gender equality, environmental sustainability, and a cooperative economy.

councils and communes elect, resulting in municipal authorities declaring people's municipalities.[30]

Venezuela

Another example of communal democracy in practice involves Venezuela. Beginning in the 1980s, partly in response to the government's corruption and brutality, towns and neighborhoods across the country formed networks of assemblies to discuss economic and social issues. Under Hugo Chávez's presidency in the late 1990s and early 2000s, the assemblies evolved into communal councils, which provided direct democratic control over some local economic production. In consolidating power, communes emerged as overarching institutions that unified local councils. As of this writing, about 50,000 communes are operating in Venezuela, especially in low-income urban barrios and rural areas.[31]

30 Michael Knapp, Anja Flach, and Ercan Ayboga, *Revolution in Rojava: Democratic Autonomy and Women's Liberation in Syrian Kurdistan* (London: Pluto Press, 2016), 107; Azize Aslan, *Anticapitalist Economy in Rojava: The Contradictions of Revolution in the Kurdish Struggles* (Wakefield, Quebec, Canada: Daraja Press, 2023), especially parts 4-5.
31 Owen Schalk, "What is the future of Venezuela's communes?" *Canadian Dimension*, December 4, 2022, https://canadiandimension.com/articles/view/what-is-

Members of the commune, who are delegates from each council, discuss and implement collective decisions on local economic issues, especially the production and distribution of the commune's products. According to multiple accounts from different perspectives, these communes represent spaces of radical democracy that move beyond capitalist economic production and the state as the locus of political decision-making.[32] Communes also take overall responsibility for assuring adequate welfare services for their members.

Venezuelan communal governance developed partly from an important advance in Marxist theory rather than the more anarchist orientation that inspired the Rojava revolution. The original conception of the socialist state, as enunciated by Engels and later elaborated by Lenin, Guevara, and others, involved a temporary condition in which an ethical transformation would occur so that moral incentives that consider the society's well-being would become stronger motivators than material incentives aiming to improve one's individual wellbeing. At that point, the socialist state would "die off" or "wither away," and the stateless condition of communism would flower. Lenin elaborated on these transitions from a capitalist state to a socialist state to communism.[33] Among the countries

the-future-of-venezuelas-communes.

32 The following sources present detailed and varying accounts of Venezuelan communes: George Ciccariello-Maher, *Building the Commune: Radical Democracy in Venezuela* (London: Verso, 2016), especially chapters 1 and 5; Cira Pascual Marquina and Chris Gilbert, *Venezuela, the Present as Struggle: Voices from the Bolivarian Revolution* (New York: Monthly Review Press, 2020), especially Introduction and Part One ("Communes and the Reorganization of Society"); Chris Gilbert, *Commune or Nothing! Venezuela's Communal Movement and its Socialist Project* (New York: Monthly Review Press, 2023), "Introduction: Putting the Commune Back into Communism," and chapters on specific communes; Chris Gilbert, "The Dream of a Thing: Refounding the Economy of a Venezuelan Commune," *Monthly Review* 76, no. 2 (June 2024), 51-66, https://monthlyreview.org/2024/06/01/the-dream-of-a-thing-refounding-the-economy-of-a-venezuelan-commune/; Schalk, "What is the Future of Venezuela's Communes?" See also note 43 below.

33 Friedrich Engels, *Herr Eugen Dühring's Revolution in Science [Anti-Dühring]*, 1877, Part III, Section II, https://www.marxists.org/archive/marx/works/1877/anti-duhring/ch24.htm; Vladimir Lenin, *The State and Revolution: Class Society and*

with "actually existing" socialism, none actually has continued to move beyond the socialist state.

A possible exception in progress is the Bolivarian revolution in Venezuela, which explicitly has aimed to move beyond both the capitalist state and socialist state. While in prison, Hugo Chávez read the work of István Mészáros, a Marxist social philosopher who fled Hungary after the Soviet invasion of 1956. Until he died in 2017, Mészáros emphasized the importance of transforming the state, which he has called "Leviathan" (echoing Hobbes), as part of the revolutionary process.[34] Moving beyond the state, Mészáros argued, is a necessary condition for moving beyond the "capital system." Beyond Leviathan, in this vision, local and regional communal organizations govern through a process of radical democracy "from below" without a formal state apparatus. Although Mészáros did not acknowledge the similarity, the ultimate goal of communal governance without a formal state apparatus resembles the goal of some anarchist or ecosocialist visions, including those of Bookchin, Öcalan, and revolutionaries in Rojava.

Chávez, who invited Mészáros to join a group of his closest advisors, prioritized the development of communes in Venezuela. Before he died, Chávez convinced Nicolás Maduro to continue prioritization of the communes as a mechanism for moving beyond the state and its determining role in a political economy based on the capital system. Subsequently, a chronic crisis resulted mainly from destabilizing interventions and

the State, Part 4, https://www.marxists.org/archive/lenin/works/1917/staterev/ch01.htm#s4; Guevara, "Socialism and Man in Cuba."

34 István Mészáros, Beyond Leviathan: Critique of the State, ed. John Bellamy Foster (New York: Monthly Review Press, 2022), especially Part Two and Appendix 4. Foster's introduction traces Mészáros's earlier work, including the importance of the "capital system" that persisted in socialist societies, as well as Mészáros's impact on Hugo Chávez and the Venezuelan revolutionary path. Mészáros's preface clarifies his allusion to Hobbes's treatment of the state in Leviathan, contrasted with other major theories of the state.

economic sanctions led by the United States but also from actions and inactions by the Maduro-led government that often weakened the communal movement. Popular discontent and ambiguous election results have reflected continuing class conflict and dialectical tensions between the communes and the state. While Maduro and other state officials have expressed support for the communes, a combination of capitalist and socialist elements of the Venezuelan state have reinforced hierarchical power, undermining the participatory processes of commune-based decision-making. Yet, despite aggressive interventions by external powers and ongoing internal struggles within Venezuela, the communes so far have persisted.

Communes have continued to accept responsibility for governance and key welfare functions, such as ensuring adequate housing, food, and health care. Regarding health care, for instance, communes and municipal governments have assumed key roles. However, due to external interventions and sanctions, plus mismanagement by state officials, the Venezuelan public-sector system with responsibilities for public health and health services has deteriorated. In addition, the Ministry of Health, as a highly bureaucratized part of the state, has blocked or discouraged some crucial programs to improve access.

In response, communes and municipalities initiated their own local health and welfare services. These efforts outside the federal government eventually led to a national program, Barrio Adentro ("community within"), in which communes and municipalities recruited doctors from Cuba to provide primary care in areas that previously lacked services. *Barrio Adentro* obtained such impressive results and popular support that the Ministry of Health eventually began to participate. During the COVID-19 pandemic, the community-based organizing in communes and municipalities led to intense, door-to-door outreach in many parts of the country, associated with relatively high vaccination rates and apparently better mortality.

More recently, Barrio Adentro has seen somewhat less success for multiple reasons, including continuing efforts by the United States to maintain economic sanctions and other efforts to impede the Bolivarian revolution.[35] In Venezuela, these intense processes concerning health care, food, housing, and other welfare functions persist despite external and internal obstacles.

Cooperation Jackson and Other Solidarity Economies

Among radical movements representing people of color, communes and democratic neighborhood assemblies have

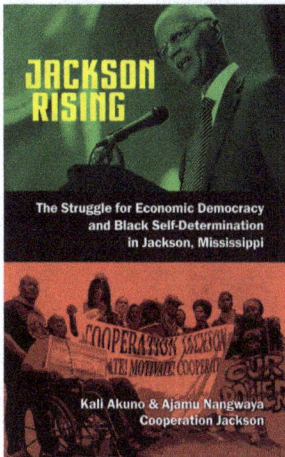

JACKSON RISING

The Struggle for Economic Democracy and Black Self-Determination in Jackson, Mississippi

Kali Akuno & Ajamu Nangwaya
Cooperation Jackson

https://darajapress.com/publication/jackson-rising

become critical for programs of justice and liberation. For Ervin, "The commune is a staging ground for Black revolutionary struggle" and a living example of how an alternative society can be organized.[36] To combat oppression under racial capitalism, the establishment of participatory democracy at the neighborhood level serves as the key basis for governance and social welfare.[37]

Cooperation Jackson in Mississippi has inspired many other organizing projects. Its revolutionary model embraces communal democracy and

---

35 Amy Cooper and Oscar Feo, "The Rise and Fall of Barrio Adentro," *NACLA Report on the Americas* 54, no. 1 (2022), 80-84, https://bit.ly/3FgvQpY; Amy Cooper, *State of Health: Pleasure and Politics in Venezuelan Health Care under Chávez* (Oakland, CA: University of California Press, 2019), especially chapters 1-3; Carles Muntaner, René M. Guerra Salazar, Joan Benach, and Francisco Armada, "Venezuela's Barrio Adentro: An Alternative to Neoliberalism in Health Care," *International Journal of Health Services* 36, no. 4 (2006), 803-11, https://bit.ly/4k1KiB9; Charles Briggs and Clara Mantini-Briggs, "Confronting Health Disparities: Latin American Social Medicine in Venezuela," *American Journal of Public Health* 99, no. 3 (2009), 549-55, https://bit.ly/4duWY1i.
36 Ervin, *Anarchism and the Black Revolution*, 126.
37 Ervin, *Anarchism and the Black Revolution*, 127.

neighborhood assemblies. The project's purpose is to support communities in transforming into a post-capitalist sustainable society. Its strategy is to organize Jackson's economy democratically through neighborhood assemblies, putting it in the hands of the Black working-class majority.[38] For Kali Akuno, the People's Assemblies of Cooperation Jackson are "vehicles of Black self-determination and the autonomous political authority of the oppressed peoples and communities in Jackson."[39]

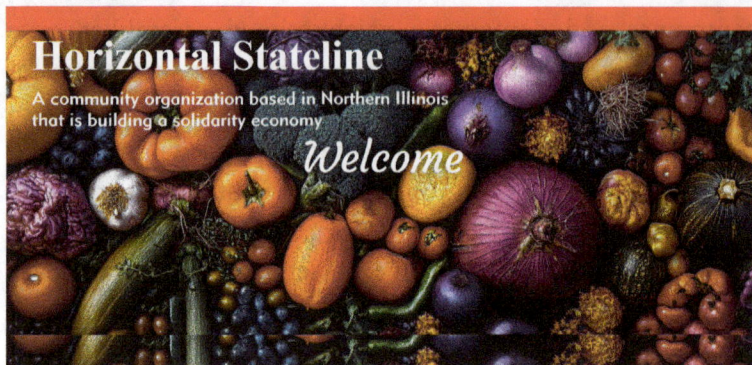

Horizontal Stateline

A community organization based in Northern Illinois that is building a solidarity economy

Welcome

https://horizontal-stateline.org/

Many groups worldwide, some strongly influenced by Cooperation Jackson, are trying to achieve revolutionary change by creating a solidarity economy outside capitalism. In the United States, over 200 organizations have collaborated in constructing such a post-capitalist economy. People in some of the poorest and most marginalized areas of the country—including Jackson, Mississippi, the Rust Belt in the Midwest, and many low-income neighborhoods of major cities—are pursuing this work with some remarkable accomplishments.

Similar organizations are growing outside the United States in areas of the world most affected by imperialism and more recent

---

38 Akuno, "Build and Fight: The Program and Strategy of Cooperation Jackson," in *Jackson Rising Redux*, 12-55.
39 Akuno, "The Jackson-Kush Plan: The Struggle for Black Self-Determination and Economic Democracy," in *Jackson Rising Redux*, 102-116.

austerity policies under neoliberalism, such as southern Europe and Latin America. These efforts often emphasize the goal of "living well" (*sumak kawsay* in Quechua, *buen vivir* in Spanish). For instance, activists in Latin American countries such as Bolivia, Ecuador, Venezuela, and Nicaragua have advanced this goal as a key component of welfare and health policies. Living well usually implies community-based solidarity and sustainability through "mutual aid," moving away from the social conditions of capitalist society that worsen poverty, inequality, environmental pollution, and unacceptable health outcomes.[40]

Most of these efforts aim to free people from spending much of their lives as workers in precarious, proletarianized jobs. In these jobs, we are unable to survive with healthy lives, let alone feel a sense of accomplishment in work and solidarity in the community. One way of describing this struggle is to reduce the need to work as "wage slaves" without the energy and time to create a new and different world. Moving into a post-capitalist world means finding solutions to some age-old problems, both related to social welfare.

First, groups trying to achieve a solidarity economy develop ways to solve the housing problem. For most people, paying for housing becomes the biggest expense, requiring us to labor for wages in the capitalist economy and also emerging as the main source of day-to-day insecurity. So the solidarity economy, first of all, finds ways to create cheap, small-scale, cooperative, pleasant,

---

40 Fernando Huanacuni Mamani, "Vivir Bien – Buen Vivir: Filosofía, Políticas, Estratégias y Experiencias Regionales," https://filosofiadelbuenvivir.com/wp-content/uploads/2013/06/Vivir-Bien-Buen-Vivir.pdf; Chris Hartmann, "'Live Beautiful, Live Well' (*'Vivir Bonito, Vivir Bien'*) in Nicaragua: Environmental Health Citizenship in a Post-Neoliberal Context," *Global Public Health* 14, no. 6-7 (2018): 923–938, DOI: 10.1080/17441692.2018.1506812; J. B. Spiegel, B. Ortiz Choukroun, A. Campaña, K. M. Boydell, J. Breilh & A. Yassi, "Social Transformation, Collective Health and Community-Based Arts: 'Buen Vivir' and Ecuador's Social Circus Programme," *Global Public Health*, 14, no. 6-7 (2018): 899-922, doi: 10.1080/17441692.2018.1504102. Regarding mutual aid, the biologist and anarchist Peter Kropotkin made important observations of mutual aid in animal societies: *Mutual Aid* (Boston, MA: Extending Horizon Books, 1914), chapters 7 and 8.

Examples of affordable housing within the solidarity economy

and comfortable housing units that require very little money, with collaborative solutions to avoid exploitative conditions, such as rent, debt, burdensome taxes, and insurance, that capitalism imposes on people who need housing. Housing co-ops find inexpensive properties in cities or rural areas where housing can be rehabilitated or constructed with increasingly sophisticated technologies that reduce the costs of labor and improve the environmental sustainability of housing materials. The aim is about US $150 per person per month of housing costs, which can be in dollars, local currency of a city or town, or non-monetary time equivalents of donated work (called by such names as "Mutual Exchange of Work" units, or "MEOWs").

Second, the path to achieving a solidarity economy includes solving the food problem. The goal is sustainable, local food production and consumption with a low carbon footprint (meaning minimum petroleum products used for fertilizers, pesticides, and, especially, transportation of food and its raw materials) and with a more favorable impact on the health of human beings, other living species, and Mother Earth.

Community gardens and food cooperatives are key components of achieving food autonomy. Gardening principles include cultivating plants that produce healthy nutrients, such as non-animal sources of proteins, with limited fats and carbohydrates. These principles recognize the worldwide epidemics of obesity and diabetes, which reflect a combination of food insecurity, "food deserts" (where healthy foods are unavailable or too expensive for purchase in many inner-city and rural areas), and over-promotion of sugar- and fat-rich foods by capitalist agricultural and food industries that produce and market processed food products. Animals for products like meat, fish, eggs, and milk products for human beings who opt for continuing non-vegetarian or non-vegan diets are locally raised, slaughtered, and packaged for local consumption.

An overall objective is independence from capitalist agriculture. Food independence means giving up consumption of food that requires access to seasonal production in distant places with carbon-based transportation over long distances, whose high financial costs and pollution contribute to climate crisis, depletion of freshwater supplies, and continuing exploitation of agricultural workers. For families of average size, the aim again is $150 per person per month of food costs, which can be in dollars or time equivalents (MEOWs).

While solving the housing and food problems both hold tremendous importance for "good living" and social welfare, several other key elements of constructing the solidarity economy beyond capitalism also deserve attention. For instance, we must replace economic activities that are ecologically unsustainable. In addition to its inherent need to exploit human beings and animals in producing goods and services for sale, capitalism also requires a continuing "expropriation of nature" in order to accumulate capital for the tiny portion of humanity at the top of society's pyramid of wealth and power. To survive and flourish through the endless accumulation of capital, the capitalist economy depends on unending economic growth. The need for growth becomes an inherent contradiction within capitalism, because growth requires the endless exploitation of natural resources that actually are limited or whose use generates problems that threaten the survival of humanity and other species. Among many examples, fossil fuels cannot last forever, and their use meanwhile generates pollution and climate change, with dangerous effects on health and well-being.

So, constructing a solidarity economy outside capitalism requires not only less growth but actually de-growth, which means stopping the vicious cycle that inherently exploits humans, animals, and Mother Earth. These changes also require shifts in desires that capitalist markets have generated. As one of many examples, each roundtrip transcontinental airplane flight generates an impact on global warming that leads to the melting of three cubic meters of arctic ice. So, we need to let go of seeing so much of the world so much of the time. Simple changes in our patterns of economic consumption, which become massive changes if enough people act on them, will reverse the unhealthy habits of growth that capitalism inherently generates.

Day-to-day life in the solidarity economy means engaging in cooperative economic activities to meet one's own needs and wants, as well as meeting the needs and wants of others in one's community. The underlying principle of such economic and social welfare activities involves mutual aid, by which people exchange goods and services without the exploitative structures and processes by which capitalism encourages a small proportion of the world's population to accumulate vast wealth. At the same time, millions suffer from poverty, precarious jobs, housing insecurity, and hunger. Interestingly, one doesn't need money for many of these economic activities.

Communities worldwide are discovering and implementing local economies that do not require much, if any, national currency, such as dollars. Instead, people are returning to more straightforward versions of economic exchange, where goods and services are produced and exchanged directly at the local level.

Several types of non-capitalist economic activities are emerging. Through barter, people can directly exchange a good or service, satisfying what each person needs or wants; barter can include welfare-oriented services such as those provided by health and mental health professionals. With time banking, a person can do one hour of work anywhere in a specified community of participants; after one person provides one hour of work, he or she can request one hour of work from the time bank, which coordinates requests for services and keeps track of time worked. Health and mental health cooperatives within communities can operate within a time bank framework: Practitioners provide services they are trained to offer and, in return, receive goods and services that they need. Communities can also create their own local currencies, which people use to exchange goods and services, including services involving health and mental health.

By participating in the solidarity economy, community members enhance the local economy and also reduce dependency on expensive and carbon-producing transportation of products and workers to and from other parts of the world. Within many communities, people decide to share their infrastructure, including tools, kitchens, libraries, workspaces, equipment, communications such as phone and internet, and buildings for housing, stores, clinics, hospitals, and other facilities that respond to everyday needs and wants. Such spaces become components of a "commons," which is available for everyone to share and contributes to everyone's welfare but does not generate profits that some people can enjoy at the expense of others.

What is the role of "electoral democracy" in the solidarity economy? Not much. Communities worldwide that are trying to construct economies not dependent on or dominated by the global capitalist system have developed a profound skepticism about the capitalist state, and this skepticism also applies to the feasibility of successful and enduring welfare systems managed by the capitalist state. As this understanding applies to elections, the focus moves from the national and state levels to the local level, usually the county or municipality. Activists take part in limited electoral work to achieve "dual power" at the local level. But they let go of illusions about elections and maintain clarity about the adverse effects of elections throughout history.

As implemented most clearly by Cooperation Jackson, dual power involves two elements of power. First, to summarize briefly, activists build a network of strong community-based organizations that focus on different components of the solidarity economy (such as housing, food, ecologically sustainable energy production and waste management, transportation, education, and health and mental health services) and that make decisions by direct participatory discussion and consensus within a "communal" structure. Adapting their model from revolutionary struggles in other countries and theories of transition beyond the capitalist state, local communes eventually assume the main responsibility for governance and providing welfare services and choose the regional leaders who implement policies shaped mostly from below.

As we contemplate developments in Rojava, Venezuela, and Mississippi, we see radical efforts to transform the democratic process, rather than remaining an aspiration, already being put into practice. These examples clarify that a realistic alternative is possible. Community-level democracy helps us understand each other's needs, reducing social and economic barriers and highlighting our similarities and the needs we all share. Such processes foster the development of meaningful post-capitalist welfare systems.

From Here to There

The community must be the focal point of political and economic decision-making in a post-capitalist welfare system. But getting to that point is likely to be transitional rather than immediate.[41] Radicalization through political education and activism becomes the foundation of revolutionary change.[42] In the process of assemblies, local gatherings organized by activists stimulate regular discussions of social and economic issues impacting our communities. Attendees highlight important issues and, through debate and discussion, create a platform that promotes communal politics and community-based solutions.

Our long-term goal is to empower the community as the source of political and economic authority while rejecting the capitalist state as much as possible. Local assemblies and communes become the heart of political and economic decision-making. As in the examples of Rojava, Venezuela, and Jackson, achieving this aim will not be an event but a process that will take time, blossoming from the initial seeds that we sow now. We can launch this process by establishing forerunners to community assemblies. They may not hold the full political and economic authority we ultimately desire, but they offer a democratic space for the community to debate local issues and collectively decide upon a course of action.

These stages inevitably involve confronting the capitalist state, particularly at the municipal level. Local assemblies

41 Symbiosis Research Collective (John Michael Colon, Mason Herson-Hord, Katie S. Horvath, Dayton Martindale, and Matthew Porges) "Dual Power and Revolution," in *Jackson Rising Redux: : Lessons on Building the Future in the Present*, ed. Kali Akuno and Matt Meyer (Oakland: PM Press, 2023), 415.
42 Eiglad, *Communalism as Alternative*, 67.

are the most direct means of achieving this confrontation. Elected representatives from each assembly represent their communities within municipal government. The representatives hold no authority to make their own decisions. Instead, their opinions on each issue reflect the collective decisions of the assembly.

Although Cooperation Jackson's long-term goal is to develop autonomous communities built upon solidarity and cooperation, far from the influence of the capitalist state, the current incarnation of its people's assemblies illustrates how an assembly operates in the initial stages of revolutionary transformation. In Cooperation Jackson, an assembly provides community members the opportunity to participate democratically in the delivery and organization of social welfare projects. Additionally, the assembly pressures municipal government and economic enterprises to support more radical change than they would otherwise. In Cooperation Jackson this process has taken various forms, including organizing protests and direct actions, but also participating in municipal politics to influence the actions of local government.[43]

To make our movement for communal democracy clearly understood, a transitional platform of policies is crucial. The platform offers policies reflecting a clear pathway from our current social and economic situation to the revolutionary destination where we want to arrive; it includes a mixture of short-term and long-term policies.[44] All policies and goals originate from within the community, not from established political parties. Members of each assembly debate and decide upon the policies and goals to pursue. Some policies support community members now through welfare services, tackling those issues that impact them on a day-to-day basis.

43 Akuno "The Jackson-Kush Plan: The Struggle for Black Self-Determination and Economic Democracy," 102-116.
44 Eiglad, *Communalism as Alternative*, 72.

Short-term benefits point the way to long-term advantages in a continuing fight for the future.

Essential to this transitional platform is maximizing the community's authority over public expenditures. A scheme of this nature closely reflects the survival program developed within the Black anarchist tradition. Developing a movement for radical change and attempting to tackle the most pressing needs, Ervin demands that government funds must be turned over to Black communities for social programs.[45] This demand deserves wholehearted support in the early stages of revolutionary transformation. A key task for each local assembly is to participate in the decision-making process and to fight for control of public funds. A transitional platform relating to welfare comprises four key components.

1. Democratic Control Over State Funds
Local assemblies democratically determine the allocation of public finances. They achieve this process by having assembly representatives in municipal government influence the actions of municipal departments and pressuring municipal governments to allow assemblies to take control of budgets and projects.

2. Community Base of Cooperatives and Mutual Aid
Supported by public finances under the authority of each assembly, an infrastructure of cooperatives and mutual aid organizations receives support in public services and small private enterprises.

3. Expanded Access to Housing
A collaborative platform uses public funds to support the growth of cooperative housing. Local assemblies influence the planning process and support the development of community land trusts that acquire land for housing.

---

45 Ervin, *Anarchism and the Black Revolution*, 132-133

4. Promotion of Community Wellbeing

Communities can foster well-being in several ways. Access to housing greatly impacts the physical and mental well-being of community members. Health care provision expands, including that relating to public health. Communal farms and food cooperatives, communal green spaces, access to program grants, and community control over public transport are essential public health and welfare policies.

In the following sections we say more about these policies. Such key policies comprise a collaborative platform. The path to radical transformation involves a succession of changes that gradually accumulate, resulting in genuine structural changes moving beyond the confines of racial capitalism. Such transformative processes are not simply wishful thinking. Movements for change ranging from Cooperation Jackson, Cooperation Humboldt, Rojava, and Venezuela to Zapatista-controlled areas in Chiapas, southern Mexico, also illustrated below, are already working to implement comparable policies. A reality of many such welfare issues is that the foundation for transformative change already exists under racial capitalism. That is, the underpinnings of a post-capitalist social welfare system need not develop from scratch; they already live in many of our communities.

From the Old, New Seeds are Sown

Describing the cooperative movement during the nine-teenth century, Marx wrote adamantly that it represented "within the old form the first sprouts of the new, although they naturally reproduce… all the shortcomings of the prevailing system."[46] For Marx it was possible for organizations and social relations that opposed capitalist values to develop from within capitalism, although they would inevitably experience challenges shaking off capitalism's imprint. Echoing this sentiment, the Industrial Workers of the World (IWW), influenced by anarcho-syndicalism, made clear efforts in their 1905 constitution to organize collectively under capitalism; each struggle opposing exploitation exemplified the establishment of a "new society within the shell of the old."[47]

The search for a new way to organize society does not have to be the sole preserve of the theoretically creative conjuring up new and imaginative ideas. Capitalism already provides the foundations of a new society, including welfare provision. A current generation of radical activists recognizes this situation, making clear: "If we want real change, should we draw up a sketch of a just society and then simply march towards it? We think it's better to look around and find the seeds of a better future – perhaps dormant – in the present and nurture them into a viable alternative that can challenge and transform the world around us."[48]

46 Karl Marx, *Capital*, volume 3 (London: Lawrence and Wishart, 1971), 440.
47 "Preamble to the IWW Constitution," Industrial Workers of the World (IWW), https://iww.org.uk/preamble/.
48 The Symbiosis Research Collective, "How to build a new world in the shell of the old," *Ecologist*, April 23, 2018, https://theecologist.org/2018/apr/23/how-build-new-world-shell-old.

Affected by both historical and current struggles of working people, many capitalist nations already contain networks of grassroots, and community-based institutions linked neither to the broader capitalist state at the national or federal level nor to the private sector. These institutions are not stifled by the administrative chains of the state or the prize of profit. They operate as community institutions under the democratic control of their members to meet community needs. Capitalist societies do not just include institutions that exclusively reflect the needs of business, despite the dominance of these institutions. We do not have to look too far to find institutions that oppose capitalist values.[49] Under capitalism, we can point to the existence of anti-capitalist spaces that reflect anti-capitalist values.[50] These are the foundations from which a progressive welfare system can develop, with a wider post-capitalist economic and social life more generally. Many of these institutions will require modification to assist with the creation of a post-capitalist welfare system. Successful social change more likely will occur if we use institutions we already have, ones with which we and most community members are already familiar.[51]

Mutual aid underpins institutions intrinsic to change. With a lineage predating the welfare state of many capitalist nations, organizations that embody the ethic of mutual aid encapsulate the historical struggles of working people to protect themselves collectively against exploitation and oppression. These instruments of popular organization, which emerged more than a century ago when working-class communities struggled against the worst excesses of an unchecked free market system, now again provide the foundation for radical transformation.[52]

49 Michael Lebowitz, *Between Capitalism and Community* (New York: Monthly Review Press, 2020), 122-124
50 Wright, *How to be an Anticapitalist in the Twenty First Century.*
51 Symbiosis Research Collective, "Dual Power and Revolution," 415.
52 Symbiosis Research Collective, "Dual Power and Revolution," 426.

Institutions of Justice and Resistance: Mutual Aid

Embracing institutions anchored in communities echoes the position of anarcho-communist Peter Kropotkin. Economic and political liberation, he argued, will have to create new forms for its expansion in life instead of those established by the state.[53] When Kropotkin was writing his last book, the working classes of many capitalist nations had already developed networks of self-help organizations based on mutual aid. The collective needs that these organizations met varied but included numerous goods, resources, and services associated with welfare. As anarchist Colin Ward asserts, mutual aid organizations provided health care and clothing, supported funeral costs, and underpinned friendly societies and building societies, among other programs.[54] As the twentieth century progressed, however, the influence of these organizations faded as the dominance of the state expanded. Our goal now is to rediscover them.

Contemporary examples of such organizations underpinned by the values of mutual aid vary, but the most prominent are co-operatives, friendly societies, community benefit societies, community land trusts, and worker-owned businesses.[55] This broad base of institutional cooperation permeates Cooperation Jackson's solidarity economy. Anchored in community-based cooperation and collectivism, the solidarity economy aims to establish a cooperative economic system.[56]

---

53 Peter Kropotkin, *Modern Science and Anarchy*, 1913, https://bit.ly/45hVeWS.

54 Colin Ward, *Social Policy: An Anarchist Response* (London: Freedom Press, 2000), 11.

55 Kali Akuno and Ajuma Nangwaya, *Jackson Rising: The Struggle for Economic Democracy and Black Self-Determination in Jackson, Mississippi* (Quebec: Daraja Press, 2017); Matthew Brown and Rhian E. Jones, *Paint Your Town Red: How Preston Took Back Control and Your Town Can Too* (London: Repeater, 2021); Jessica Gordon Nembhard, *Collective Courage: A History of African American Cooperative Economic Thought and Practice* (University Park, PA: Pennsylvania State University Press, 2014); Mary N. Taylor and Noah Brehmer, eds., *The Commonist Horizon* (Brooklyn, NY: Common Notions, 2023).

56 Howard Waitzkin, Alina Pérez, and Matthew Anderson, *Social Medicine and the*

As Kali Akuno makes clear, the solidarity economy of Cooperation Jackson consists of, and is looking to develop further, "a network of cooperative and mutually reinforcing enterprises and institutions, specifically worker, consumer, and housing cooperatives, and community development credit unions as the foundation of our local solidarity economy."[57] All these organizations offer an opportunity to harness the collective strength of communities so that every one of us can have our needs met without the precarity of our economic circumstances threatening our well-being.

Accepting the importance of mutual aid in the formation of a post-capitalist society, we need to ask: what exactly is it? Its essence is that of a group of people who work together to provide resources for a specific need. This approach fosters unity among participants by recognizing shared needs and the benefits of group action above individual efforts. It is an anti-authoritarian method, which starkly contrasts with the history of state welfare provision. Mutual aid organizations are emancipatory rather than solely a means of resource provision. They support participants to assert themselves in demanding their rights and dignity, thereby promoting awareness of social justice.

As Pandemic Research for the People (PREP) asserts, mutual aid organizations operate to educate individuals as well as provide for them. Opposing capitalist principles, these organizations make clear the exploitative and anti-democratic power structures of capitalism and the unequal distribution of resources and opportunities.[58] Reflecting collectivism

....
Coming Transformation (New York: Routledge, 2021), chapter 10.
57 Kali Akuno, "The Jackson-Kush Plan: The Struggle for Black Self-Determination and Economic Democracy," in *Jackson Rising Redux: Lessons on Building the Future in the Present*, eds. Kali Akuno and Matt Meyer (Oakland: PM Press, 2023), 106.
58 Pandemic Research for the People, *Moving Beyond Capitalist Agriculture: Could Agroecology Prevent Further Pandemics?* (Quebec: Daraja Press, 2021), https://darajapress.com/publication/moving-beyond-capitalist-agriculture, https://mronline.org/2021/08/01/moving-beyond-capitalist-agriculture-could-agroecology-prevent-further-pandemics/

and democracy, organizations underpinned by this ethic are fundamentally different from capitalist institutions, which reinforce individualism, selfishness, competition, and suspicion of others. Mutual aid offers us a valuable means of organizing ourselves so we can oppose capitalism and agitate for progressive change.

The possibilities offered by mutual aid to deliver welfare have become widely recognized over the last decade. Austerity and cuts to welfare in many capitalist nations have resulted in mutual aid intervening to support and organize welfare in an environment where the capitalist welfare state has enthusiastically withdrawn its engagement.[59] This collective principle allows us to access resources and services that often would be unattainable if we pursued our welfare needs individually. Mutual aid offers an opportunity for fair and equal access to welfare services. As anarchist Emma Goldman asserted, individual freedom gains strength through cooperation. "Only mutual aid and voluntary cooperation," she made clear, "can create the basis for a free individual and associational life."[60]

59 Joel Izlar, "Radical Social Welfare and Anti-Authoritarian Mutual Aid," *Critical and Radical Social Work* 7, no. 3 (2019): 349-66.
60 Emma Goldman, *Red Emma Speaks*, ed. A.K. Shulman (Amherst, MA: Humanity Books, 1998), 118.

A Post-Capitalist Welfare System

An efficient welfare system allows us to reach our full potential while removing the artificial hurdles and disadvantages imposed by racial capitalism and the harm caused by exploitation, oppression, and discrimination. Looking ahead, we see how a post-capitalist welfare system can be organized and governed. Drawing on current and historical examples of efforts to offer alternative welfare provisions distinct from the state, we consider housing, health care, and income maintenance programs as examples.

Housing as a Cooperative Opportunity

Having a home is a fundamental human need. A sense of security about housing, regardless of economic volatility, is crucial for our well-being. Under capitalism, however, many of us do not experience this sense of security. Market requirements and rising inequality have forced an increasing number of people to live in insecure conditions. Housing is a foundational pillar of any post-capitalist welfare system, where it no longer functions as a commodity under the private ownership of individuals. Instead, housing becomes a community asset, collectively owned. Collective ownership ensures that all members of the community are able to obtain a home. No longer is housing primarily understood as an investment or financial asset. Rather, a home is a place to live.

The most equitable way to organize housing in a post-capitalist welfare system and to reflect the values of communal control is to expand cooperative housing. Housing coops already have become widespread in many capitalist countries, although they are not the primary method of providing housing. For the working class, cooperative housing has helped meet housing needs without depending on the state and the market. Not all cooperative housing schemes are alike. Some common methods of providing this form of housing involve tenants cooperatively administering their homes owned by individuals, organizations, or municipalities. In a more radical scenario, tenants become communal owners.

In a post-capitalist welfare system, individuals join a housing coop to qualify for tenancy in one of its homes. After joining as a coop member, everyone becomes an equal share-holder. There are no individual property owners. Rather, the cooperative collectively owns all the homes.[61] Through membership, tenants become able to take part in collective decision-making about the coop's management. Membership comes with an obligation to support the coop. Such support involves voluntary labor to repair the properties, maintenance of common spaces, and helping develop educational, recreational, and creative programs.

Examples of a more radical approach to housing that we are proposing emerge from the British cooperative housing movement. While still a minority form of housing, squeezed between private construction and municipally owned housing, the coop housing movement in Britain has aimed to achieve accessible housing as part of a post-capitalist welfare system.

For half a century, the Sanford Housing Co-Operative in southeast London has successfully fostered key values of the cooperative approach. The coop's members collectively own and manage fourteen properties, including communal gardens, lawns, ponds, and organic vegetable plots, free from market interference.[62] This arrangement constitutes communal property, which the coop democratically controls.

Likewise, the Coventry Peace House in Coventry implements

61 John Hands, *Housing Co-operatives* (London: Castleton Publishers, 2016), 36.
62 "About Sanford," Sanford Housing Co-operative, https://sanford.coop/about/.

the principle of community ownership. Renters simultaneously act as cooperative members and collective owners for all properties. Each member serves as the custodian of their respective property. Many residents of the Coventry Peace House actively engage with social issues in the community, promoting radical causes, including pacifism and social justice.[63]

Reflecting a vision of the coop as an organization that provides education and services, Kindling Housing Cooperative, established in 2016 in Oxford, requests that coop members make decisions democratically and manage the organization under a common ownership agreement. While collectively delivering housing for its members, Kindling does so with an overt political mission. The coop encourages members to be socially and politically active as they pursue a non-hierarchical organization and try to ensure ecologically sustainable practices.[64]

The potential of cooperative housing as an alternative to private landlords, where residents take control of their own housing needs, has emerged as a widely supported goal in fights for liberation among people of color. Housing coops organized through neighborhood assemblies and local communes, Ervin asserts, become a fundamental part of a broader struggle for self-determination.[65] In Cooperation Jackson, Max Rameau argues housing is a human right, but this principle contradicts the idea that under capitalism housing is a commodity. Overcoming this contradiction, Cooperation Jackson embraced the goal of removing housing and land from the market so they could become protected goods. A key component of Cooperation Jackson's housing agenda is to purchase properties with the sole intention of forming cooperatives as part of a wider goal to establish communal home ownership.

---

63 "About Us," Coventry Peace House, https://coventrypeacehouse.wixsite.com/coventry-peace-house/.
64 "About Kindling," Kindling Housing Cooperative, https://kindlingcoop.org.
65 Ervin, *Anarchism and the Black Revolution*, 143.

Cooperative housing offers the community a means to develop and own their own homes, allowing all the opportunity to access affordable and secure accommodation.

An additional component of Cooperation Jackson's housing agenda includes collective ownership of land. Although still at an early stage, community ownership of land has become a key objective of the Fannie Lou Hamer Community Land Trust (CLT) in Jackson. Cooperative ownership and management lead to the removal of land from investors' speculative gaze. Instead, the land trust protects land for the sustainable and collective development of new homes and housing cooperatives. The serious pursuit of a collective means of providing housing depends on removing land from the clutches of private capital and firmly placing it in the hands of the community. CLTs have become indispensable for developing affordable housing under community ownership. Rameau argues, "As decommodified land, those properties are liberated to serve their more important social functions of housing human beings... and providing common space."[66]

66 Max Rameau, "The Jackson-Kush Plan: The Struggle for Land and Housing,"

Financing for initial construction and purchase of properties can come from several sources. Current examples of cooperative housing schemes illustrate a possible role for the government in this process. Uruguay, which is arguably the principal example of radical cooperative housing in Latin America, has witnessed units of government evolve as a primary source of loans for communal housing. Relinquishing reliance on government and fighting for the community to become the heart of political and economic authority is the ultimate objective. But, with revolution seen as a process rather than an event, as already made clear, we can realistically begin with communities increasing collective control over the municipal government and harnessing its influence for the common good. Controlled by mutual aid banking societies, credit unions, and community development corporations, Ervin argues, government funds are utilized for the construction of occupant-controlled housing as part of a transitional agenda.

Using the government to finance cooperative housing is a short- to medium-term option in a transitional platform. But, autonomous sources that do not rely on the state are essential. Acting in solidarity, a fundamental strategy involves the pooling of finances by existing cooperatives granting loans to new cooperatives, which allows them to purchase and develop properties. Housing confederations can institutionalize such a system. As a principal way of developing regional networks of cooperatives, members of housing confederations can share advice, information, and resources. Of equal significance, the confederations provide a forum for the collective voice of the cooperative housing movement.

Established during the late 1980s in Britain, an example of a successful housing confederation is Radical Routes. Its members are multiple housing cooperatives whose combined

....
in *Jackson Rising Redux: Lessons on Building the Future in the Present*, eds. Kali Akuno and Matt Meyer (Oakland: PM Press, 2023), 275.

objective is to help build new housing cooperatives while also uniting the movement. Radical Routes provides possibilities for its members to act in solidarity by pooling their resources to fund new housing ventures collectively. The goal is to manage a continuous and repeatable process of gathering resources for expansion. Radical Routes' primary goal through this strategy is to criticize capitalist housing arrangements and to demonstrate mutual aid as an alternative.[67]

Radical Routes provides an existing example of how collective action, free from the interference and dominance of the capitalist state, can support the development of housing under the collective control of those who live there. Other sources and activities to raise revenue include those that come from ethical small business practices that do not involve exploitative practices of racial capitalism. Member cooperatives and confederations can increase revenue through productive activities, particularly using CLTs. Profits from farming, food production, composting, recycling, handicrafts, and other ethical enterprises, as part of the solidarity economy, will lead to reinvestment for social development, including new housing. Through what the Symbiosis Research Collective identifies as a community Common Fund, which absorbs a proportion of profits generated by community-wide mutual aid initiatives, revenue can be pooled and reinvested in social infrastructure.[68]

Community Health Care and Prevention

Founded on the ideals of cooperation and solidarity, the examples of housing show that a real alternative is possible. Although overshadowed by the monolithic private sector, within those spaces relatively free from capitalist values, there are attempts to organize welfare in a way that empowers the community and helps ensure that everyone gets their basic

67 "Housing without Landlords," Radical Routes, https://www.radicalroutes.org.uk/.
68 Symbiosis Research Collective, "Dual Power and Revolution," 425.

needs met. In a welfare system suitable for a post-capitalist society, health care also shows this potential for fundamental change. First, it is important to clarify what we mean by health in a post-capitalist society.

When asked what we understand by good health, people likely refer to feeling physically healthy. Being free from disease, pain, and physical discomfort usually means being healthy. It is difficult to argue against the experience of good physical health as essential to our experience of being healthy. But, rather than primarily a physical phenomenon, in a post-capitalist society our understanding of health, and specifically good health, must have more depth.

A post-capitalist understanding of health means wellbeing. Including our physical experiences, wellbeing involves a holistic understanding of health. This idea recognizes that good health also includes our mental and emotional state, as well as acknowledging that good health is not just something that is found within us.[69] Rather, good health greatly depends on a supportive social context. In the "social determination" of health, social environments and experiences impact our bodies.[70] With well-being at the heart of post-capitalist health policy and healthcare delivery, attention focuses on not only the physical health of individuals but also emotional health and

69 This formulation of health follows the traditional definition of the World Health Organization: "Health is a state of complete physical, mental and social well-being and not merely the absence of disease or infirmity." World Health Organization, "Constitution," https://www.who.int/about/governance/constitution. Also pertinent are the concepts of buen vivir, discussed earlier, and social determination in social medicine, discussed further below.

70 The works of Nancy Krieger on "ecosocial theory" and Jaime Breilh on "critical epidemiology" provide crucial research and analyses of social and ecological determination: Nancy Krieger, *Ecosocial Theory, Embodied Truths, and the People's Health* (New York: Oxford University Press, 2021) and *Epidemiology and the People's Health: Theory and Context*, 2nd edition (New York: Oxford University Press, 2024); Jaime Breilh, *Critical Epidemiology and the People's Health* (New York: Oxford University Press, 2021). Contributions in social medicine analyze the historical roots and contemporary applications of these perspectives concerning the impact of social context on health and illness: Waitzkin, Pérez, and Anderson, *Social Medicine and the Coming Transformation*, chapters 1-4.

healthy social circumstances. Social, economic, and political factors become paramount in shaping our physical and mental health, including the well-being of the wider community.[71]

This understanding reflects the orientation of social medicine based on extensive practice, research, and analysis over the past two centuries. Inspired by Frederick Engels, Rudolf Virchow, and Salvador Allende, among others, our approach recognizes that political ideology and economic organization impact both good and poor health through social determination.[72] Exploitation, oppression, and discrimination exert a profound impact on the distribution of poor health and well-being. While access to clinical interventions and services is important, an essential post-capitalist goal is to ensure that our communities and broader society are organized and function healthily.

What characteristics of society promote health and well-being? As previously stated, access to secure, high-quality housing is critical to our well-being. Additionally, adequate income serves as a foundation for an individual's health and well-being. Healthy food, access to green space, meaningful work, and a strong social network are also crucial. Communities that foster love and respect promote cooperation and solidarity and create organizations reflecting these values. Thus, the welfare system outlined here is fundamental to optimal health and well-being.

Beyond the wider social determination of health, a focus on health-related services and organizations reveals that mutual aid can serve as their basis. But unlike housing, where examples of cooperative provision already exist, the same cannot be said of cooperative health services. The relative scarcity of cooperative health organizations partly reflects the large role of national governments in funding and organizing the delivery of health care.

71 Lee Humber, *Vital Signs: The Deadly Costs of Health Inequalities* (London: Pluto Press, 2019)
72 Waitzkin, Perez, and Anderson, *Social Medicine and the Coming Transformation*, 24-44.

The increasing role of the state in the provision of health care after World War II offered undeniable benefits to those of us and our families who have used such systems, receiving free or heavily subsidized support. Limitations of state healthcare systems in wealthy nations, however, have become clear. State-funded and controlled national health programs usually operate in deficit mode, with insufficient numbers of professionals, levels of capacity that do not meet demand, and inadequate resources in technology and equipment. Notably, state systems operate with a hierarchical structure that largely reflects the wider class structure of society. These systems usually lack sufficient financial investment and suffer cutbacks and privatization during and after economic crises as the state acts to protect threatened industries and financial institutions.

For these reasons state systems commonly have experienced challenges and barriers to sufficient delivery of health care in communities. Over the last forty years, they have faced threats and attacks linked to neoliberal principles and frequent efforts to remodel health care in the image of the market. Moreover, to varying degrees, state health care has operated under a centralized model. Despite the deterioration of provision, these programs have remained bureaucratic, under the administrative control of state officials, with service users disempowered and lacking authority or a sense of control and ownership. A post-capitalist health care system, therefore, decentralizes services and locates them within communities that take control of their delivery.

Community health care frequently emerges as a focus of organizing, reflecting the oppressed position and marginalization affecting people of color. Recent history demonstrates that in the fight for economic and political emancipation, communal means of meeting the community's healthcare requirements have become fundamental to the emancipatory agenda. The 1970s witnessed organizations such as the Young

Lords Party (YLP) establish community-controlled healthcare programs. A socialist-inspired civil rights organization located in Chicago and New York, the YLP fought the oppression and exploitation of Puerto Ricans and other Latinos.

The YLP committed itself to the ideal of self-emancipation. Advocating community control of health services, it strived to establish community clinics. Embracing the principles of health promotion and education, members of the YLP developed community health programs such as tuberculosis screening, vaccination campaigns, and rubbish collection. With existing health services and municipal government failing to serve these communities sufficiently, the YLP initiated its own community-based actions.[73]

During the same period, the Black Panther Party (BPP) launched similar projects. People's Free Medical Clinics, for example, provided free treatment to members of the community.[74] For each clinic a volunteer team included doctors, nurses, and medical students. BPP leaders emphasized locating the clinics in the heart of disadvantaged communities. Funding came from the communities, relying on donations from local businesses and residents. The programs engaged directly with communities through mobile units that provided primary care and preventive services. Important examples involved testing for sickle cell anemia and providing vaccinations. Other health programs included the People's Free Ambulance Service and, recognizing the importance and neglect of nutrition, initiatives such as free breakfast programs for children and food programs for other community members. Offering vital services, each of the BPP's survival programs also demonstrated an educational purpose. Showing the benefits of community-based programs, one goal was to raise awareness among community members

73 Darrel Enck-Wanzer, *The Young Lords: A Reader* (New York: New York University Press, 2010), 188-201.
74 Alondra Nelson, *Body and Soul: The Black Panther Party and the Fight against Medical Discrimination* (Minneapolis: University of Minnesota Press, 2011), 75-114.

For the Black Panther Party, revolutionary change would come from the collective effort of the community, such as community social programs like their free breakfast clubs for children.

about the high quality of these services compared to private and state-run provision.[75]

More recent examples of post-capitalist health care emerged from the Zapatista movement in Chiapas, southern Mexico. The movement adopted a strategy of civil resistance that mostly ignored government authorities and rejected public services, including health care and education, as provided by governmental institutions. The Zapatistas' civil resistance has not recognized the powers of the state. They implemented this decision at a high social cost since they rejected benefitting from rights that other Mexican citizens enjoyed. Instead of collaborating with the state, Zapatista communities have initiated their programs, including local health centers, new schools, and training programs.

Despite limited resources, the Zapatistas continue to build a community-based approach to health care that does not rely on the capitalist welfare state or the private medical sector.

75 Dr. Huey P. Newton Foundation, *The Black Panther Party: Service to the People Programs*, ed. David Hilliard (Albuquerque, NM: University of New Mexico Press, 2008).

Pursuing the goal of democratic control, the autonomous organization of healthcare has characterized Zapatista-controlled regions. Composed of healthcare workers, including outreach workers, reproductive health specialists, and vaccinators, as well as residents of each community, autonomous regions have established local healthcare committees (LHC) that have allowed community health needs to be identified and debated. The LHCs have provided a focal point of each community's healthcare provision, with health care providers and users cooperating in the delivery of services. In addition, there is direct political representation of LHCs on regional health committees, with the latter having the responsibility for overseeing the provision of health care regionally and supporting equitable delivery of services among all municipalities and communities.[76] A strong collaborative and democratic ethos permeates the delivery of health care, with its provision situated at the heart of the community and the health care agenda determined collaboratively between health professionals and community residents.

Many communities have initiated health houses to ensure that the community remains the focus for the delivery of health services. Directed by health promoters, health houses serve as the initial points of contact to meet healthcare needs. Volunteers selected by a community for the role receive education to meet the community's health requirements. Health promoters play an essential role in fostering good health, as preventive medicine has become a key priority in Zapatista health care.

The development of community health workers (CHWs) in Cooperation Humboldt shares similarities with Zapatista health care. As part of the community, CHWs support

---

76 Among accounts of Zapatista health services in Spanish, the following study is helpful also for English readers: J.H. Cuevas, "Health and Autonomy: The Case of Chiapas, A Case Study Commissioned by the Health Systems Knowledge Network," 2007, https://web.archive.org/web/20211123184551/https://www.who.int/social_determinants/resources/csdh_media/autonomy_mexico_2007_en.pdf.

residents, assisting them in their access to health services and delivering health education. CHWs are not medical experts, but they come from the same community as the people they serve. They have similar needs and identify with the community. This sense of solidarity is used to break down boundaries, allowing CHWs to help people meet their needs. CHWs' contributions flow from the principle that, as members of the community, they not only require care but also can care for others. For Cooperation Humboldt, the community becomes a vital location for the provision of health and well-being, where ordinary people feel more empowered to take control of their own health and to support the health of others.[77]

A desire to democratize the provision of health care also characterizes the revolution taking place in Rojava. Beginning with each local commune, members of the commune assess the health care needs of the community through debate and discussion. From there, representatives of each commune meet at the level of the neighborhood council, which analyzes the overall health needs of each commune under its jurisdiction in a report. Representatives of each neighborhood council then submit this recommendation to district-level health assemblies, which implement policies and initiatives.[78]

Expansion of communal health care, like other parts of a post-capitalist welfare system, takes time. One key target involves community control of state health spending. Rojava offers an example of what is already possible. Once established, local assemblies fight to take control of state expenditures for health care and public health services. With communities making autonomous decisions about public funds, community health programs like those already illustrated can flourish. Social movements involving the Young Lords and Black

77 Cobb, Engelke, Lopez, MacFarland, McKee, Miller, Mogollon, Munoz, and White, "Cooperation Humboldt: A Case Study," 327
78 Knapp, Flach, and Ayboga, *Revolution in Rojava: Democratic Autonomy and Women's Liberation in Syrian Kurdistan,* 185-189.

Panthers in the 1960s and 1970s and the Zapatistas, Rojava, and Cooperation Humboldt in more recent years all have shown that a transformative approach to capitalist health care emerges with communities taking control of decision-making. These initiatives demonstrate the possibilities when communities pursue communal forms of health care. In these ways, the process takes many aspects of healthcare delivery away from the state and, instead, integrates them within communities.

These examples from many places around the world show communities already creating new mechanisms to meet critical healthcare needs. These and other examples show how community-based healthcare services can develop within post-capitalist welfare systems. A consistent highlight of such systems involves selecting people within the community to assist others with their healthcare needs. This process provides spaces for community members to educate themselves about health issues and to gain democratic control over decision-making.

Income Maintenance

Marx argued vehemently in the *Economic and Philosophic Manuscripts of 1844* that labor should be a fulfilling experience, allowing individuals to express themselves freely, both physically and mentally. Workers should be able to relate to what they produce as meaningful expressions of their essence and inner creativity. Work we enjoy and find meaningful is beneficial to both our physical and mental well-being. But many of us have firsthand experiences of work under racial capitalism that are far from this favorable experience. It can be tedious, monotonous, stressful, and, in some situations, dangerous.

In post-capitalist situations, work remains the primary source of monetary income for most people, although conditions become radically different. Echoing Marx's perspective, the alienation and oppression of work transform into an experience that provides us with greater meaning and

purpose. Crucial to this change is the development of a solidarity economy where work and production focus more on
meeting needs and enhancing the well-being of the community. Although the solidarity economy presents the basis of
a post-capitalist economy, even under this system, some
community members, friends, and family are unable to work.
Childhood, old age, sickness, disability, caring responsibilities
for a loved one – such circumstances make it difficult to work.
For those not working, we accept a collective, moral obligation to support them. Although we have identified existing
post-capitalist methods of delivering housing and health care,
major challenges emerge for any system trying to offer an
income not contingent on working for a living. These challenges emerge from the practicalities of generating an income
stream under capitalism separate from labor or the state's
own, often punitive, social security provision. We can, though,
support and gain inspiration from the idea of a universal basic
income (UBI).

Paramount to any post-capitalist welfare system is
assuring that those of us who are not working still receive a
sufficient and regular income. UBI offers various advantages.
As a source of income not related to work, it takes the place
of existing social security support. As well as helping the most
vulnerable and needy, UBIs offer us all, regardless of whether
we are working or not, a choice to withdraw from the workforce entirely, accepting an opportunity instead to engage in
voluntary community service. Anyone accepting this role will
qualify to receive UBI as a means of financial support instead
of earning a wage. No longer participating in work, we are
free to contribute to the community, engaging in voluntary
efforts to support the growth and prosperity of the community
and its members. This support takes several forms, such as
helping to establish social clubs, organizations, and networks,
visiting isolated members of the community, assisting in the

maintenance of public spaces, or representing the community in municipal government, among other initiatives.

Under racial capitalism, the insecurity and precarity that many wage earners experience mean that, despite possible good intentions, they do not have the time or capacity to devote themselves to the community. The security and guarantee of a regular income not linked to work can liberate us. Not dependent on work to earn a living, UBI offers us a chance to pursue activities and interests that support our emotional and intellectual growth as well as the well-being of community members.

Experiments with UBI schemes offer some indication of how this arrangement works and its impact. Piloted in Finland in 2018, the Finnish example illustrates that an unconditional guaranteed income positively impacts well-being. It reduces feelings of anxiety, insecurity, and stress, while recipients also develop a more positive attitude towards their economic well-being and a greater sense of autonomy. Moreover, it offers some an opportunity to engage in activities that they previously were unable to do, or could not devote as much time to, including voluntary work and caring for family members.[79]

Evaluations of UBI programs in other countries have led to similar favorable results. In Spain, where a UBI experiment took effect in 2017, observations with participants indicate that a guaranteed income exerts a positive impact on life satisfaction and mental health. A precursor to UBI piloted in Dauphin, Manitoba, Canada, from 1974 to 1979 demonstrated positive consequences. Those who received UBI showed enhanced physical and mental health, as well as greater social interaction and engagement with the community.[80]

79 Ibeing Economy Alliance, "Finland: Universal Basic Income Pilot," May 2020, https://weall.org/resource/finland-universal-basic-income-pilot.
80 Evelyn L. Forget, "The Town with No Poverty: The Health Effects of a Canadian Guaranteed Annual Income Field Experiment," *Canadian Public Policy – Analyse de Politiques*, 37, no. 3 (2011), https://www.utpjournals.press/doi/full/10.3138/cpp.37.3.283.

Financing, administration, and implementation of UBI take place mainly at the municipal and regional levels, as in the last two examples. The operation of UBI programs devolves to the community level, as policy decisions happen in the same communities where recipients of this support reside. The "means test" that determines whether recipients' incomes and assets are small enough to qualify for assistance – so often a harsh, degrading, and punitive experience under racial capitalism – ends. As communities become more autonomous, financing for UBI flows from communities themselves, which generates funding for UBI mainly from local solidarity economies. Local assemblies exert authority to raise income via contributions from individuals and businesses. Confederal or regional councils exercise similar income-raising powers but with the authority to redistribute income among local assemblies based on local needs.

Looking to the Future

The role of welfare is fundamental in moving beyond racial capitalism. But among the issues of economic justice, wealth distribution, racial discrimination, patriarchy, and environmental sustainability, among many others, welfare often remains overlooked. Under racial capitalism, organized welfare has always occupied a contradictory position. Aiding the development of productive workers who can be exploited and functioning as an instrument of social control, the welfare state frequently has benefited racial capitalism, even as many economic and political elites have characteristically objected to it publicly.

Yet, despite this contradictory position, capitalist welfare states often display qualities and principles that oppose capitalist values despite many efforts to suppress them. As Erik Olin Wright observed, many welfare services historically have offered spaces in opposition to capitalism, manifesting values of collectivism and universalism.[81]

---

81 Wright, *How to be an Anticapitalist in the Twenty First Century*, 103.

The very principle of welfare contrasts with capitalist values of individualism, competition, and self-reliance, which is why welfare systems have remained so tightly controlled. The primary goal for all of us who want to create a just and equal society free of division is to establish what an alternative welfare system looks like and how to work toward it.

Fundamental to the creation of a post-capitalist welfare system, we have argued, is situating it within communities under democratic control. For a welfare system to meet our genuine needs, especially those of society's most vulnerable, the new system delivers and administers services as closely as possible to all users. Community members determine democratically how the post-capitalist welfare system delivers services and what services it delivers. Rather than a service and system that we experience as something done to us and as a distant institution at best, the new welfare system fosters a sense of empowerment among people who use welfare services. Given the responsibilities of a post-capitalist welfare system – housing, health care, income, education, among much more – having a sense of empowerment about the welfare system's impact on us and others is vital.

The success of community-organized, post-capitalist welfare depends on community politics. Building the new welfare system also involves withholding consent to the exploitative and unsuccessful welfare system of the capitalist state.[82] As our examples in Jackson, Rojava, Venezuela, and elsewhere illustrate, the process of moving welfare systems beyond capitalism starts with a communal structure of direct democracy with limited connections to the capitalist welfare state. After

82 Howard Waitzkin, *Rinky-Dink Revolution: Moving Beyond Capitalism by Withholding Consent, Creative Constructions, and Creative Destructions* (Wakefield, Quebec, Canada: Daraja Press, 2020), https://darajapress.com/publication/rinky-dink-revolution-moving-beyond-capitalism-by-withholding-consent-creative-constructions-and-creative-destructions; and (New York: Monthly Review Essays, 2020), https://mronline.org/2020/05/19/rinky-dink-revolution/.

laying the foundations for communal politics, the long-term objective is to eclipse the state with communal institutions of local and regional governance evolving as the primary sites of democracy, assuming responsibilities previously enacted inadequately by the capitalist welfare state.

Obstacles of power and privilege, those brandished by economic and political elites and by the capitalist state that supports them, will always obstruct, often retaliate against, and frequently attempt to co-opt and subsume movements and ideas perceived as threats. Through both ideology and force, elites and the state strike back and try to subdue opposition to capitalism. But in the face of such hostility, as our examples make clear, the fight for a humane, post-capitalist society and welfare system has begun in many places throughout the world. Already, these efforts to oppose capitalism, to counter its exploitation and oppression, offer viable and lasting models of post-capitalist welfare. The ideas and organizational foundations are already in place. Efforts to make such changes can succeed. So, as the creators of Cooperation Jackson advise, now is the time for "building the future in the present."[83]

---

83 *Jackson Rising Redux: Lessons on Building the Future in the Present,* eds. Kali Akuno and Matt Meyer (Oakland: PM Press, 2023).

David Matthews is a lecturer and course director for the undergraduate program in Health and Social Care at Bangor University, Wales. His writings focus on welfare, the welfare state, and welfare-related social policy issues such as health, mental health, housing, and disability. Growing up in a working-class family who relied upon the welfare system as both a means of support and to provide opportunities, David is acutely aware of the necessity of welfare to improve people's lives and the need to develop a system that meets the real needs of working people. A new book, *The Class Struggle and Welfare: Social Policy under Capitalism*, was published by Monthly Review Press early in 2025.

Howard Waitzkin is a distinguished professor emeritus of health sciences and sociology at the University of New Mexico, USA, and practices internal medicine part-time in rural areas. Partly reflecting his upbringing in a low-income, working-class family, he has been active in struggles to expand access to health and welfare services in the United States and Latin America. He is the author of *Rinky-Dink Revolution* (2020) and *Social Medicine and the Coming Transformation* (with Alina Pérez and Matthew Anderson, 2021), among other books, and co-edits the pamphlet/manifesto series, "Moving Beyond Capitalism – Now!"

MOVING BEYOND CAPITALISM – NOW!

Moving Beyond Capitalism—Now! represents a collaboration between Daraja Press and *Monthly Review* magazine.

The aim is to publish and distribute brief, easy-to-understand publications that present concrete proposals/manifestos for revolutionary actions that will help us move beyond the global capitalist political-economic system. See **https://bit.ly/43mEVW8**

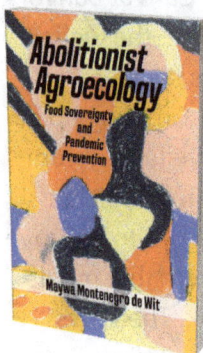

Abolitionist Agroecology, Food Sovereignty and Pandemic Prevention

Pandemics have their roots in the violent separation of communities from their territories, seeds, knowledge and wealth. Racism enables such theft as fundamental to capitalist expansion.

To tackle pandemics and food injustices, Maywa Montenegro calls for an abolitionist agroecology.

ISBN 978-1990263-03-3

Also available in Spanish

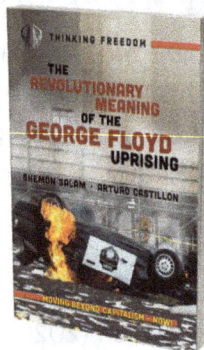

The Revolutionary Meaning of the George Floyd Uprising

In an effort to think through the experience of the uprising and prepare for the great struggles that are coming, *The Revolutionary Meaning of the George Floyd Uprising* provides an in-depth analysis of what exactly happened during the 2020 uprising, its potentials, internal limits, and strategic implications.

ISBN 978-1-988832-95-1

Also available in Spanish

Rinky-Dink Revolution: Moving Beyond Capitalism

This pamphlet tackles the question: how do we get from A to B, capitalism to post-capitalism? Rinky-dink revolution involves actions and inactions that are easy, safe, mundane, unglamorous, and feasible within every person's life.

ISBN 978-1-988832-53-1

Also available in Spanish and Korean

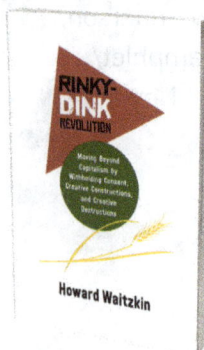

EU Safety Information
Publisher: Daraja Press, PO BOX 99900 BM 735 664
Wakefield, QC J0X 0C2, Canada
info@darajapress.com | https://darajapress.com
EU Authorized GPSR Representative:
Easy Access System Europe, Mustamäe tee 50, 10621 Tallinn, Estonia,
gpsr.requests@easproject.com
For EU product safety concerns, please contact us at info@darajapress.com

www.ingramcontent.com/pod-product-compliance
Lightning Source LLC
Chambersburg PA
CBHW052142270326
41930CB00012B/2985